All
About

by
Oliver R. Selfridge
Illustrated
by
Jerry Joyner

◆ *Addison-Wesley*

Text Copyright © 1978 by Oliver Selfridge
Illustrations Copyright © 1978 by Jerry Joyner
All Rights Reserved
Addison-Wesley Publishing Company, Inc.
Reading, Massachusetts 01867
Printed in the United States of America
ABCDEFGHIJ-WZ-798

Library of Congress Cataloging in Publication Data

Selfridge, Oliver.
  All about mud.

  Includes index.
  SUMMARY: A discussion of the uses, sources, and
characteristics of mud, a useful and often poetic
substance loved by man and beast.
    1. Mud — Juvenile literature. [1. Mud]
I. Joyner, Jerry. II. Title.
QE471.2.S43   553'.6   76-30399
ISBN 0-201-07448-6

Table of Contents

This is a book all about MUD. This book will tell you different things about MUD, what you can do with it, how to make it, and so on. It may tell you more about MUD than you care to be told, but you can always skip the dull parts (although I don't think there are any) or the parts that tell you things you don't want to know. It's called "ALL ABOUT MUD," but perhaps it ought to be called "ALL ABOUT MUD THAT I KNOW OR COULD FIND OUT," because I'm sure there is lots more about MUD that I haven't put in.

About this Book

What MUD is

MUD is usually brownish or blackish, but in some parts of the country it can also be yellowish or reddish (not all at once). It squishes in the hands without feeling too slimy. MUD is supposed to be very bad for shoes, which have to be cleaned after getting MUDdy, but it is supposed to be good for women's faces, which sometimes are cleaned with the help of MUD packs at beauty parlors.

Lots of good things are MUDdy — they look like MUD, feel like MUD, or move like MUD — at some time or other. Before it is cooked, Chocolate Cake batter should be like thick MUD. The bottom of Turkish coffee should be all MUDdy. Cement just mixed should squish through your fingers like MUD.

MUD is dirty — wonderfully dirty. It ought to be dirty, because it isn't MUD unless it's dirty. If someone ever tries to give you clean MUD, look at it very carefully; it probably isn't MUD at all.

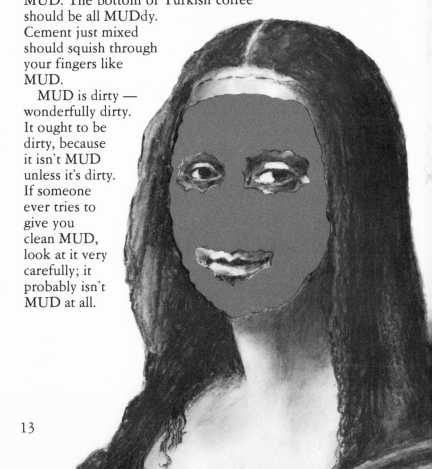

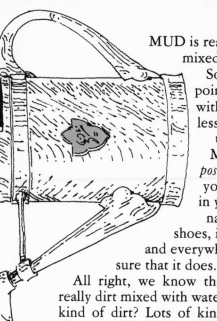

MUD is really just dirt mixed with water. So there is no point in playing with MUD unless you expect to get dirty. MUD is *supposed* to get on your clothing, in your finger-nails, on your shoes, in your hair, and everywhere. Make sure that it does.

All right, we know that MUD is really dirt mixed with water. But what kind of dirt? Lots of kinds, but not every possible kind. You can't use the dirt on a dirty tee-shirt you wore when you oiled your bicycle, or the dirt from a vacuum cleaner to make MUD; but you can use most dirt that you find on the ground.

A good place to start looking for MUD is in your yard or garden after a good rain. If it hasn't been raining, make your own rain shower with the hose or a watering can.* Sprinkle lots of water right in the dirt. Then mix the dirt with the water; squishing it

---

*If it is too cold for rain, or if the dirt is frozen, as it often is in the North in winter, you can still do several things: the first is to wait till spring, which is easiest, but takes the longest; the second is to go somewhere where it is much warmer and start again; the third is to dig up some frozen dirt and bring it into a warm place like a house.

with your fingers or toes, or both, is the best way.

If you happen to live where there is a lot of water and not very much dirt, like on a boat, collect dirt in a bucket and pour water into the bucket, as I said before. If you don't use enough water, you will have a mixture that is stiff, called "wet dirt." That is not the same thing as MUD at all; add more water at once. If you don't use enough dirt, or if you add too much water, you will have a mixture that is called "dirty water," a kind of MUD soup, not good for much. Add more dirt at once, if you have enough.

Now, *generally,* if the MUD is too stiff, you add more water, and if it is not stiff enough, you add more dirt. It is very hard to take away extra water if you have added too much.* And it is also very hard to take away extra dirt. So you have to get it right, making it just as stiff as you want it to be. A lot depends on the kind of dirt you have, and how much there is of it.

Usually the dirt underneath trees and flowers is good for making MUD. In fact, if that kind of dirt is wet from rain or snow, it may *be* MUD already.

Another good place to find good MUD is the bank of a stream or river. This kind of dirt usually comes already mixed with water, too.

---

*You can wait while some of the water evaporates, of course; but you have to be sure and stir it occasionally while that is happening, because otherwise the mud will crust over on the drier surface and still be too wet underneath.

15

How **MUD** *acts*

Bricks and Water

WOODEN FRAME

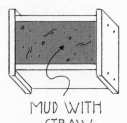

MUD WITH STRAW

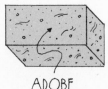

ADOBE BRICK

I have already told you that MUD has water in it. The oldest kinds of bricks were made by drying the water out of the right kind of MUD in the sun or over a fire, so that it baked and became hard. You have to use the right kind of MUD for that; sometimes people would add straw to it as well. The bricks made this way were sometimes called "adobe."

In some ways MUD acts like *water,* and in some ways it acts like *bricks*.

You can lift a *brick* with your bare hand.

You cannot lift *water* with your bare hand, at least, not very well.

How about MUD?

You can pour *water* from a pitcher bit by bit, making the bits very tiny.

You cannot pour a *brick* from a pitcher bit by bit at all.

How about MUD?

You can throw a *brick* very easily.

You cannot throw *water* very easily, without using a hose or a cup or something.

How about MUD?

You can count *bricks*.

You cannot count *water*.

How about MUD?

You can make a pile of *bricks*.

You cannot make a pile of *water*.

How about MUD?

You can walk on a *brick* path.

You cannot walk on *water*.

How about MUD?

There are lots of ways that MUD isn't like either *bricks* or *water*.

You cannot squish *water* through your fingers, because it won't stay in your hand long enough. You cannot squish a *brick* through your fingers, because it is too hard. You *can* squish MUD through your fingers. It oozes slowly and sometimes it goes GLOOP on the ground.

If you drop a *brick* on the ground, it bangs or clunks, and then lies still, all in one piece. But when a *brick* is dropped by a very tall person, or by any person at a window on the third floor, say, it may break into several pieces.

If you drop *water* on the ground, it splashes and trickles and spreads all over.

But if you drop MUD on the ground, it plops and splatters and slurps, but then it stands quivering in little piles. You cannot paint a sign with *water,* because it has no color and just makes things wet. You cannot paint a sign with a *brick,* because it is too hard; its color does not come off. But you *can* paint a sign with MUD, and it is a good thing to do, too.

Bricks don't make things dirty. Sometimes, of course, *bricks* are dirty themselves, but that's not the same thing.

Water makes things wet, but it doesn't get them dirty. In fact, *water* used with soap often gets things and people clean.

If you want to make something really gloriously dirty, just about the quickest and best way is to use MUD.

Things MUD is Like

Chocolate Pudding

Some other stuffs are much more like MUD than bricks are or water is. One of the hardest to tell from MUD is

In several ways, Chocolate Pudding is frighteningly like MUD.

You can squish Chocolate Pudding through your fingers or toes, or both; it goes GLOOP, just like MUD.

When Chocolate Pudding is found in a garden, it looks just like dark brown MUD. In the same way, when dark brown MUD is served for dessert, it looks just like Chocolate Pudding.

Chocolate Pudding stirs just like MUD with a spoon or a stick.

If you drop Chocolate Pudding on the ground, it plops and splatters and splurps and quivers in little piles, just like MUD.

If you bake Chocolate Pudding in the oven long enough, it dries out and turns hard and crumbly, just like MUD.

If you dip your finger in Chocolate Pudding, you can smear your initials on the back of your other hand or on a paper napkin, or on your knees, just like MUD.

Perhaps you are thinking now that it is a pretty good thing that MUD is not often found in dessert bowls, and that Chocolate Pudding is rarely seen in gardens, because they look alike and feel alike and sound alike. But there is an easy way to tell them apart.

No, it isn't the smell. When it is cold, neither MUD nor Chocolate Pudding has much smell. Smell does work well when they are hot. It's taste. Chocolate Pudding and MUD just don't taste the same. Most grown-ups don't think that tasting MUD is a good idea. But children outside in their backyards or gardens taste MUD, by accident, all the time, and it doesn't seem to hurt them very much. Actually, most MUD doesn't taste very good at all.

Here is a true story about MUD tasting. Some time ago, a 5-year-old boy called Peter dug a hole, about as large as a medium-sized sauce pan, in his front yard. He then went into the kitchen and made four packages of chocolate pudding, and then he poured all the pudding into the hole. A short time later when his father came home from work, there was Peter, sitting by a hole at the side of

the driveway, about to put a spoonful
of thick brown gooey stuff into
his mouth.

"What on earth are you doing,
Peter?" his father asked.

"I'm seeing if this stuff tastes like
Chocolate Pudding."

"Nonsense," his father said, "that's
MUD. Don't put it into your mouth.
You don't find Chocolate Pudding in
a hole in the garden."

Peter didn't answer, but for dessert that night he gave his father a bowl of chocolate pudding. When his father had finished it, Peter asked him, "How did you like the MUD?"

"That wasn't MUD," Peter's father replied. "That was Chocolate Pudding. You don't find MUD in a dessert bowl."

"But you were the one who called it MUD. I got it from the hole I was

sitting beside this afternoon."

Peter's father went and looked in the hole and tasted the brown gooey stuff in it. And it *was* Chocolate Pudding. So he told Peter he was sorry and he had been wrong.

But you don't find Chocolate Pudding in the garden very often. If you do, however, you will notice that even garden variety Chocolate Pudding tastes very different from MUD.

Whipped Cream

Fresh Cement

Whipped Cream is much easier to tell from MUD than Chocolate Pudding is.

Whipped Cream squishes through your fingers just like MUD, and stirs sort of just like MUD, and plops just like MUD when you drop it.

But . . . Whipped Cream is white. Also it doesn't taste a bit like MUD. So, if you see a strawberry shortcake with white MUD on top, taste it. You will probably find that it is not white MUD at all, but Whipped Cream. If you fill a hole in your garden with Whipped Cream, it still won't look or taste like MUD. Your parents will tell you one other important difference from MUD — Whipped Cream is very expensive.

In fact I have never seen MUD as white as Whipped Cream, and I have never heard of any either.

There is no doubt about it. Fresh Cement is very like MUD. Cement is slightly stiffer than real MUD, and it's usually lighter in color. If you rub Cement on your clothes, it leaves a grey mark instead of the brown of MUD. But you can get just as dirty with Cement as you can with MUD.

The only really reliable way to tell Cement and MUD apart is to wait a while. After a day, more or less, MUD will be dry and crumbly (providing it hasn't been raining), but Cement will be hard and rocklike. If you write your name in fresh Cement, then when the Cement has hardened, your writing will have hardened too.

24

It will be there FOREVER, or at least as long as the Cement is.

So now we know that it is always safe to write "This is not MUD" in pale-colored stuff that may be either MUD or Cement. If the stuff hardens, the message is right, and it will always be right. If the stuff doesn't harden, the message will be wrong, but it will already have crumbled or washed away, and disappeared the way every mistake should.

The first thing to say is that *Things to Do with MUD* don't have to be useful like building a skyscraper, passing a school examination or making a speech. In fact, probably the best things to do with MUD at the beginning are not very useful at all, but just feel good, like walking barefoot along a MUDdy dirt road in the country: it has stopped raining, the sun is shining, you are in no particular hurry, it is warm because it's summer — and there may even be fresh blackberries on the bushes alongside the road. At least, that's the way I remember the last time I was on Block Island, which is between Long Island, part of New York, and Cape Cod, part of Massachusetts.

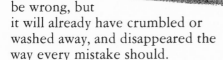

*Things
to do with*

MUD

Sitting outside making MUD pies feels pretty good, too. For MUD pies, the MUD ought to be little stiffer than for MUD soup. Gardeners use MUD soup for planting new plants that friends have given them or that they have just bought from the nursery. They dip the roots in MUD soup so that they won't dry out while the holes are being dug. Plant roots love MUD. Of course, plants don't feel or think the way people and animals do, but if they did, I suppose they would lead pretty happy lives with their feet in MUD.

If you want to bake play-cookies made from a stone or pebble, the thing to do is dip it into MUD so that it is covered, and then dip it into sand, so that the sand sticks to the MUD and makes an outside coating like sugar. It is hard to hold the cookie without leaving bare spots from your fingers. Parents and other people who

cook do the same things often, using beaten eggs instead of MUD and real sugar instead of sand. They often have difficulties with leaving finger marks.

If your cookie is made of just MUD, then you don't need to dip it into MUD at all, but you can just sprinkle it with sand. MUD for cookies has to be a little stiffer even than for pies, in order for it to stand up properly on the plate.

There are several useful things that people do with MUD. People who drill oil wells sometimes use MUD to help the drills work better. It does several things at once: it helps to cool the drill heads, which can get very hot grinding against the rock; it can help to lubricate the parts of the drill, and it can carry away the bits of rock that have been ground away by the drill. The MUD is sent down one pipe in the middle of the drill and back up another.

I mentioned on page 16 that bricks made from MUD were called "adobe." In many parts of the world they still use adobe bricks for houses and other buildings. Since the adobe is usually not baked hot enough to be as hard as a regular brick, it will wash away a little in a hard rain. In Iran many of the buildings have brick roofs like that, and in order to protect the bricks the people put more MUD on top of them. When the MUD becomes thin from rain, the people remark to each other that it is time to reMUD the roof, and they spread more MUD over the old. In most places where sun-baked MUD is used for building, straw is added to the MUD and it makes it much stronger; the straw acts as a reinforcement, like the steel in reinforced concrete.

People who make telescope mirrors use a kind of MUD to make them smooth and exactly the right shape. The MUD is made from a kind of finely ground rock. The finest, which is the last one used on the mirror, is called rouge, because it is like the powder used to make cheeks red, if anybody wants red cheeks (rouge is French for red). The ground rock is mixed with a little water or sometimes oil.

Here are some things you can do easily with MUD:

If the MUD has a lot of clay in it, you can probably bake it so that it becomes hard; perhaps the sun will be hot enough, but the kitchen stove is probably quicker. The easiest way is to put what you want to bake onto aluminum foil and then into the oven. The MUD has to be quite stiff. You can add straw to the MUD before you bake it, as people do who use MUD for building, which I mentioned above. As a matter of fact, any kind of thread will do if it has some strength. It shouldn't rot, and so grass won't last long. If the thready stuff is very soft, like cotton or nylon, find some way to stretch it out, so that it doesn't become all curled up, because then it won't add any strength. The most interesting question is what to bake. An obvious answer is pots and other kinds of pottery, but I am sure you can think of many other things.

You can use MUD easily to make a trail for other people to follow; just drop splashes of MUD on the ground or on walls or trees. The MUD will dry up and blow away in a few days, or else it will wash away in the rain, so that you don't have to wait for years to do it again. If it is very hot in summer, and the MUD is cool, you can give yourself a MUD coat. MUD is better than water, because the water runs off. Of course, the MUD will warm up pretty fast in the sun. I have seen pictures of elephants in Africa doing this to keep cool.

You can use MUD to keep your hair in place, if it is not too long, but long enough to blow around in the wind.

If you have enough MUD in a sort of trench, you will find it is the best stuff to stick sticks into to make a fence. Often dirt is too hard to do that with.

If you can find MUD of different colors, you can make a MUD painting. The colors will change as the MUD dries out.

Fill a flat pan with MUD, and let it dry out slowly. The MUD will shrink a little as it dries and make a beautiful design of cracks. If the MUD is put in the pan a little deeper, or if it dries out faster, the patterns will be different.

You can probably think of other things to do with MUD yourself. Here are a few ideas to get you started:

As mosquito protection.
For disguise.
For throwing at enemies whom you don't really want to hurt.
For keeping track of where people go in the dark by following their MUDdy footprints. Of course, you have to get them to step into some MUD first. For hiding valuable things from enemies in.

Finding MUD is often more a question of when than where. Just after a heavy rain is a good time, or after a lot of snow has melted in gardens or on dirt roads. Dirt roads are really especially good places to look for MUD. A few years ago I made the mistake of thinking I could drive a car through the MUD on a dirt road just after a very heavy rain. It was certainly wonderful MUD. Deep, too. It didn't quite come in the car windows, but that was because I had closed them half-way before I climbed out of one.

Swamps and marshes are full of MUD, and they usually have lots of plants that like to live in MUD, like reeds, pickerelweed, loosestrife, and so on. Flood sites are also good places to find MUD, like the Mississippi and Nile river valleys. Spring is the best time for MUD along the Mississippi valley. The Nile floods when the rainy season has started in Ethiopia, which is in July or August.

People don't usually like the MUD from floods. During the 1966 floods in Florence, Italy, MUD destroyed millions of dollars worth of great paintings and decorations. In Torrington, Connecticut, whole factories were ruined from the MUD that filled them in a great flood in 1955.

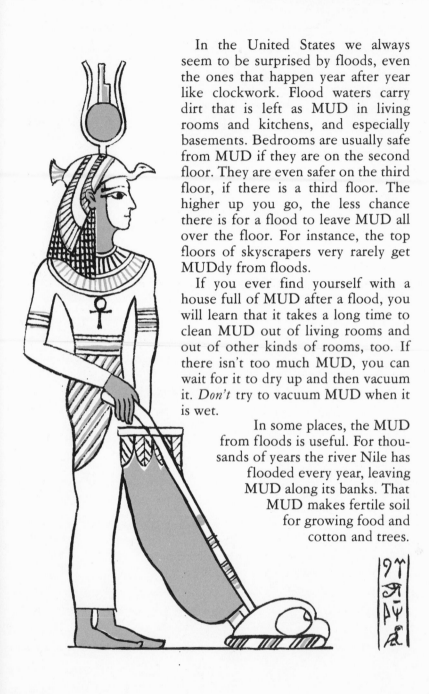

In the United States we always seem to be surprised by floods, even the ones that happen year after year like clockwork. Flood waters carry dirt that is left as MUD in living rooms and kitchens, and especially basements. Bedrooms are usually safe from MUD if they are on the second floor. They are even safer on the third floor, if there is a third floor. The higher up you go, the less chance there is for a flood to leave MUD all over the floor. For instance, the top floors of skyscrapers very rarely get MUDdy from floods.

If you ever find yourself with a house full of MUD after a flood, you will learn that it takes a long time to clean MUD out of living rooms and out of other kinds of rooms, too. If there isn't too much MUD, you can wait for it to dry up and then vacuum it. *Don't* try to vacuum MUD when it is wet.

In some places, the MUD from floods is useful. For thousands of years the river Nile has flooded every year, leaving MUD along its banks. That MUD makes fertile soil for growing food and cotton and trees.

Recently a giant dam, the ASWAN dam, has held back the flood waters, so that there is a good deal less MUD in Egypt than there used to be.

Even MUD which is good for growing cotton and food and trees is not very good for living rooms.

Animals that like MUD

Another good place to look for MUD is on the East Coast of the United States in MUD flats. MUD flats are beaches covered with MUD instead of sand; at high tide they are covered with seawater too. Clams live in MUD flats a few inches down. They wear a hard shell, called a clam shell, so that they can tell the difference between themselves and the MUD. Clams have little tubes like soft soda straws, called siphons, which they poke out into the seawater. Clams suck seawater through the siphons and sift out tiny seawater goodies to eat. When the tide goes out, they sit and think about the next high tide until someone happens by, thinking about clams or just squishing the MUD through his toes. Then the clams panic and squirt water out their siphons, making brief little fountains on top of the MUD. Of course, anyone who sees those little fountains knows just where to dig for those clams.

It is also nice on a warm summer's day to walk across a MUD flat where

clams live, when the tide is half in and half out and there are perhaps two or three feet of seawater over it. Then you can dig cautiously for the clams with your toes. When you catch one, you can save it for eating or else scratch your initials on it as a kind of brand, or scratch a short notice, like "BEHAVE" or "PLEASE DON'T EAT ME."

There is a big kind of clam that lives in New England MUD called a Quahog.* I have caught quahogs with my toes, but I ate them as chowder and didn't write any messages on them. Young quahogs are called cherrystone clams and are very good to eat raw.

A really giant clam called a GEODUCK (pronounced GOOEY-DUCK) lives in MUD flats on the coast of Oregon and Washington. It lives several feet down in the MUD instead of several inches, and it is as large as a healthy pumpkin. In fact, geoducks are too large to fit inside their shells, and they bulge out like egg salad out of and egg salad sandwich or children who grow too fast for their clothes. Geoducks are also hard to catch.

Clams are very tasty to eat, but sometimes they are a little MUDdy

---

*Pronounced KO-HOG; although some say KWO-HOG. The word is also spelled QUA-HAUG, and came from the language used by the Rhode Island Indians.

inside when they are caught. The clam sellers clean their clams by letting them sit in fresh seawater before they sell them. Clams taste better without MUD.

Many more things live in MUD than just clams. The bigger ones, which I shall talk about later, are more interesting to us perhaps because we can see them easily. But scientists think that life started in MUD, though they are not sure when, and they certainly don't yet know how. Today, MUD from the bottom of a pond is just full of tiny life or microbes.* Microscopes were invented by a man from Holland called Anton Leeuwenhoek, and one of the first things he looked at was MUD from the bottom of a pond. Probably that MUD looked pretty much as it did hundreds of millions of years ago, full of microbes and other small living things.

Of course, there is no way to be sure of that, since most microbes have such soft bodies that they don't make very good fossils. But with the right kind of MUD and the right weather, sometimes the MUD can harden and preserve whatever happens to be in it. That is how we know the most about dinosaurs; we dig the remains of their bones out of hardened MUD, which

---

*The word "microbe" comes from two Greek words, the first meaning tiny, as in microscope, and the second meaning life, as in biology.

has been buried for millions of years. Sometimes the MUD has hardened with the dinosaurs's footprints, rather like cement; so I suppose that MUD was the first cement in the world.

It is still true today that lots of animals like MUD and live in it. The big animals seem to enjoy it more; think of elephants and hippopotamuses playing in MUD. But small animals make a lot of use of it. In the cold winters in the North, frogs sleep, or hibernate, all winter in the MUD at the bottoms of ponds or ditches or lakes, without needing to breathe air, because there is enough oxygen in the wet MUD around them to go through their slimy skins.

Some other kinds of weather, bad for animals, make them take shelter in MUD. In Africa there are some kinds of fish that live in streams that often dry up; for those fishes, bright sunny days are bad weather. Then they burrow down into the MUD for protection, and just curl up and wait. Some of them have learned to breathe air, instead of water like most fishes; breathing air slowly, they can wait for years in the MUD, until the next rain softens the MUD, makes the stream flow again, and lets them swim about as usual.

In the United States, muskrats make tunnels in the MUD along the

sides of streams; they make their nests at the ends of the tunnels. Crayfish do the same and sometimes use old muskrat tunnels to save themselves the work of tunneling in MUD.

There are several kinds of wasps, like the MUD dauber or MUD wasp, that build nests of MUD. The female wasp searches for MUD and carries it to where she uses it to build a nest. The sun or maybe just the heat of the summer dries it for her and then she lays her eggs in it.

There are lots of fishes that like to eat plants at the bottom of MUDdy lakes and ponds. When they are eating, they make the water MUDdy, of course, which means that they cannot see very well. Fishes like that have often grown whiskers, so that they can feel the bottom, rocks in their way and so on. Catfish are an example of fish that have whiskers for that reason.

Many animals use the MUD at the bottoms of ponds and brooks to hide in, either from other animals that are waiting to eat them or that they are waiting to eat. A MUD puppy is a kind of salamander that likes to hide in MUD. Some insect larvae hide in MUD hoping that something will swim by that can be caught and eaten. Sometimes even small fishes are caught and eaten that way.

Unfortunately for the animals that hide in MUD, some birds search through MUD for them, which is fortunate for the birds, I suppose. The MUD dipper is a kind of duck that does that; so does the woodcock, which has a long thin beak just right for poking in MUD.

Talking about MUD

The word MUD is quite an old word and originally meant something to do with bogs and swamps.* The meanings of words change as time goes by. "Muddle" started out by meaning what the word "MUDdy" means when we talk of "MUDdying the stream," but now MUDdle means just to stir and mix in a messy way, even if there isn't any dirt around to make MUD. My desk is often a MUDdle.

If people call something MUDdy, they usually mean that it is bad in some way. If you say of someone "his name is MUD," that means that he has a bad reputation and is not to be trusted, and so on. In political fights, when two people are running against each other for Senator or Mayor or School Committee, if one says something bad about the other, that is said to be "MUD-slinging," or "dirty politics."

To "MUDdy the water" means that someone is making something confusing and hard to understand that might otherwise be clear and easy to understand. And if you say of some explanation given about something that it is "as clear as MUD," that means it is not clear at all.

---

*My dictionary tells me that originally it was the same word as "moss," which grows in bogs.

Writing about MUD

It is just possible that there *may* be one or two things that you would like to write about MUD that I haven't written here. In that case you should write them down; please send me a copy if you feel like it.* There is no way to tell you how to write, because that depends on what you have to say, how you feel, the people you are writing for, and so on. The thing to do is just to start. Lots of people worry about spelling and punctuation and paragraphing; those things are important, because they often make writing easier to read and understand, but they are not nearly as important as having something interesting to say.

There are several people who have written poems about MUD, and here are some:

E.E. Cummings was a poet who lived in the first half of the twentieth century, and in a poem called "in Just" he wrote

in Just-

spring   when the world is mud-luscious. . .

which is a wonderful way of putting it. Incidentally that small piece of the poem has the only instance in this book where the word MUD is written in lower case letters; that is

*You can write to me at my publisher:
Oliver G. Selfridge,
c/o Addison-Wesley,
Reading, Massachusetts, 01867

40

because E.E. Cummings wrote his poetry very carefully to take advantage of upper and lower cases, so that they are more than just to be heard — they are also to be seen.

Rupert Brooke was a young English poet when he was killed in the first World War. In his poem "Heaven" you may read

. . . One may not doubt that, somehow, good

Shall come of water and of MUD. . .

But more than mundane weeds are there,

And MUD, celestially fair. . .

A very famous American poet called Robert Frost wrote a poem called "Two tramps in MUD time," about a New England farmer who is visited by two tramps who want food or work; of course the time is spring, when the melting snow makes a great deal of MUD around the place.

A young poet from Utah, Carol Lynn Pearson, has written a poem called "On Nest Building," which starts

MUD is not bad
for nest building
MUD and sticks
And a fallen feather
or two will do
And require no
reaching. . . .

How to help friends who don't have enough

MUD

Probably you have enough MUD where you live. Perhaps you have some friends who don't. In that event, you can make their lives brighter by sending them a MUD kit, so that they can make MUD themselves. It may be that you are the one who does not have enough MUD. In that event, you can ask your friends to send you a MUD kit for yourself.

There are three kinds of MUD kits.

The first is for people who don't have dirt, or who don't have the right kind of dirt, but who do have water. Such people may live in New York City or in the middle of Greenland, which is all snow and ice. Put some of your best dirt in a strong paper bag, and tape it shut all the way across. Don't use staples, because some of the dirt will come out of the holes made by the staples. The dirt should be quite dry or the paper may tear. Put the bag in a strong cardboard box with the instructions: Mix with Water. On the box stick a label: MUD KIT #1.

The second is for people who don't have water, but who do have dirt.

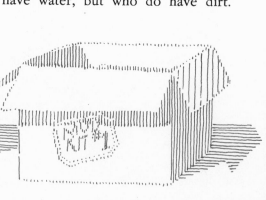

They might live in the Sahara Desert or the Mojave Desert or just about any desert where the dirt isn't just sand. Get a preserve jar, the kind used for canning jams or vegetables at home. Fill it with water, put the top on, and put it into a strong cardboard box with lots of scrumbled newspapers around it, so that it won't break. Also put in the instructions: Mix with Dirt. Put on the box a label: MUD KIT #2.

The third is for people who don't have either dirt or water. I can't think of where they might be, unless they were stuck up on a balloon or were astronauts. But if there *are* any, and they need MUD, take a MUD KIT #1 and a MUD KIT #2 and tie them together, and put on a larger label: MUD KIT #3.

The only kind of people left are people who do have dirt and who do have water. They don't need anything at all, and they probably have as much MUD as they need. However, they might not know how to make MUD, so that you should send them just the instructions from KIT #1 and KIT #2.

How was MUD discovered

Once upon a time, the whole world was very clean, and there was no dirt anywhere. You would think that everybody would be very happy, but actually not everybody was.

Caroline was frowning, because she wanted to disguise herself in the woods, so that birds and chipmunks and dragons would not notice her while she watched them. She needed something to make her clothes all dirty, and her socks and shoes and face and hands and hair. But there was no dirt anywhere to be found.

Caroline's mother was *very* sad, because Caroline's father had given the whole family a beautiful new washing machine for a Christmas present, and there were never any dirty clothes to put in it. What could she wash?

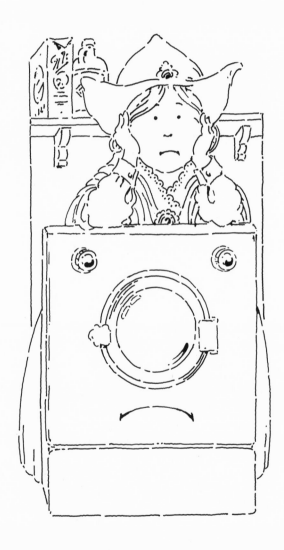

Caroline had a brother Ethan. He wasn't really happy or unhappy. He was looking for a way to make MUD pies, and of course there wasn't any such thing as MUD, because there wasn't any dirt. He and Caroline were outside looking under trees and in the garage and over by the stream at the bottom of the yard, but there wasn't any MUD at all.

They sat on the edge of the stream watching the ripples playing with each other and going off down the stream; all except for one ripple, which wobbled over a rock about an inch below the surface of the water.

Caroline reached into the water. "I think that I will give that ripple some help," she said. And she took the rock out from under the ripple.

"There he goes," shouted Caroline. She happily squeezed the rock in her hand. After a second or so of squeezing, the rock burst with a little "tssss," and Caroline's fingers were covered with MUD, the first MUD that the world had ever seen.

"What is that?" asked Ethan, and he reached out and touched her hand. His hands became covered with MUD, too.

"I'm not sure," said Caroline, "but I think it is MUD. Look." She touched the tip of her nose, and of course it became covered with MUD. Ethan laughed and laughed.

"Put some on *your* nose," said Caroline, "so that I can see how it looks. It's very hard to see mine properly, unless I cross my eyes."

Instead, Ethan gave himself two more eyebrows made of MUD and a large MUD moustache, and Caroline laughed and laughed. And she made herself a MUD beauty spot in the middle of her forehead.

But Ethan was paying no attention to Caroline. Looking at his right hand, which was covered with MUD, he brought it up to his shirt and put it on flat, and when he took his hand away there was a large MUDdy hand on his shirt.

"Oh, Ethan, you have made your shirt wonderfully dirty." And Caroline made her shoes and socks wonderfully dirty too. "Let's go home and show mother."

"We haven't finished yet," he said.

A little while later, they walked to the back door of their house and rang the bell. They were beautifully covered with MUD from head to toe, from hair to shoes, except for some holes in the MUD where their eyes, noses and mouths were.

Presently their mother came to the door, opened it and stared at those two large piles of MUD, which she had never seen before. When she realized that they were Caroline and Ethan, she gave a cry of joy.

"Oh, children, how wonderful! How wonderfully dirty you are! I will call your father so that he can see you too. Come hug me, and I'll become all MUDdy too."

So Caroline and Ethan hugged their mother and their father, and soon they were all covered with MUD from hair to shoes.

"I like the feel of MUD, but I don't like the taste of MUD," said their father, who had forgotten to leave a hole for his mouth.

"I think I will wipe my hands before I cook supper," said their mother. "Tomorrow you must change your clothes, and I will take all the dirty ones and put them in the beautiful new washing machine and get them clean." She was quite ecstatic.

And Caroline and Ethan promised to get MUDdy whenever they felt like it, and their parents could use their new washing machine happily every day afterwards.

Actually, that is only one version of how MUD was discovered. If you hear of, or think of, a better version, you should write it down, so that history books will get it right. Send me a copy if you like (use the address on page 40).

The last chapter

The world is MUDdier and dirtier than we like to admit. If a spaceship filled with Venusians were to land on this planet, it would probably land on dirt or MUD,* instead of on a clean place. It's hard to find clean things outside — clean like kitchen counters or laundry.

But children learn while they are very young that most people believe that it is bad to be MUDdy or dirty. But being dirty isn't bad and being clean isn't good; also, of course, being dirty isn't good and being clean isn't bad, either. One difficulty with believing that MUD and dirt are bad is that it makes it easy to believe that people who deal with dirt or MUD aren't worth as much as other people, so that a person who digs ditches or has to shovel manure may be regarded as not as good as other people.

Billions of years ago life started in MUD, nobody knows exactly how. Living things can't stay alive easily if things are too clean, that is, sterile or antiseptic That's why, for example, the instruments a surgeon uses have to be very clean indeed, so that there are no extra living things on them like germs that might cause infections. Most parts of the outsides and insides of living creatures are more MUDdy than sparkling clean. Blood is filled with many kinds of blood cells that take care of our bones and flesh; blood is really a kind of living MUDdy soup. The only parts of me that I can think of that are truly clean are my eyeballs; I suppose that is why people say jokingly over drinks "Here's MUD in your eye!"

Of course, it's not just in insides and outsides that the world is MUDdy. Most ways of behaving and thinking are not cleanly good or bad, or right or wrong; instead they are both and other things as well. Real arguments about important matters almost always have to be MUDdy, because they depend on the differences in what people like and value, and those differences help to make people people. If it is thought that most things are just right or just wrong, it is easy to be very sure about what to do, but history has shown us that that means it is very easy to be very sure about doing things that hurt and destroy people and civilization. It is perhaps better to try to understand how MUDdy situations are than to be sure about them.

I don't get much time these days to squeeze MUD through my fingers, and so I have written this book for children who might have the time. You should see how differently it squeezes from peas or bricks or bottle caps or paper. I hope that when you grow up you will remember what fun MUD is for children, and what fun it can be for grown-ups too, if they remember.

---

*That is, if it didn't land on water, because the surface of the earth is three quarters water. By the way, what does it mean to say "land on water?"

Acknowledgements

Page 40 "in Just" by E. E. Cummings. From *Complete Poems 1913–1962* published by Harcourt Brace Jovanovich, Inc. Used by permission from Harcourt Brace Jovanovich, Inc. and MacGibbon & Kee Limited/Granada Publishing Limited.

Page 41 "On Nest Building" by Carol Lynn Pearson. From the book *The Flight and the Nest,* by Carol Lynn Pearson, published by Bookcraft. Copyright © 1975 by Bookcraft, Inc. Used by permission.

Page 41   "Heaven" by Rupert Brooke

Index

About the Author

Oliver Selfridge hopes readers of *All About Mud* will become infected with the joy of playing with ideas, taking them to ridiculous extremes at times, in order to learn the powers and limitations that ideas have. Mr. Selfridge has published three other children's books, *Trouble With Dragons, Fingers Come In Fives* and *Sticks*. When he is not writing, he works as a computer scientist and mathematician; when he is not working, he enjoys gardening, shoveling snow, good company and late nights.

Photo by Ken Pate

Jerry Joyner has been a high school student at Corvallis High School, Corvallis, Oregon; an art student at the California College of Arts & Crafts; a designer at *Esquire Magazine*; an illustrator at Push Pin Studios, and a bookmaker on a Greek isle where he and Remy Charlip co-created the award winning book, *Thirteen. All About Mud* was designed and illustrated in an enchanted valley in the south of France.

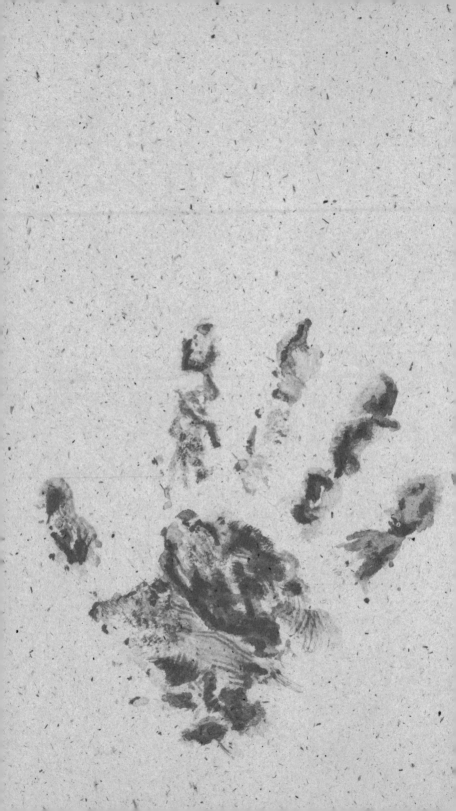